How To Use This Study Guide

This five-lesson study guide corresponds to *"How To Defeat the Giant You Are Facing" With Rick Renner* (**Renner TV**). Each lesson in this study guide covers a topic that is addressed during the program series, with questions and references supplied to draw you deeper into your own private study of the Scriptures on this subject.

To derive the most benefit from this study guide, consider the following:

First, watch or listen to the program prior to working through the corresponding lesson in this guide. (Programs can also be viewed at **renner.org** by clicking on the Media/Archives links or on our Renner Ministries YouTube channel.)

Second, take the time to look up the scriptures included in each lesson. Prayerfully consider their application to your own life.

Third, use a journal or notebook to make note of your answers to each lesson's Study Questions and Practical Application challenges.

Fourth, invest specific time in prayer and in the Word of God to consult with the Holy Spirit. Write down the scriptures or insights He reveals to you.

Finally, take action! Whatever the Lord tells you to do according to His Word, do it.

For added insights on this subject, it is recommended that you obtain Rick Renner's book

Spiritual Weapons To Defeat the Enemy or other titles, including *Sparkling Gems 1* and *2*. You may also select from Rick's other available resources by placing your order at **renner.org** or by calling 1-800-742-5593.

TOPIC

It's Time for You To Fight

SCRIPTURES

1. **1 Samuel 17:1-3** — Now the Philistines gathered together their armies to battle, and were gathered together at Shochoh, which belongeth to Judah, and pitched between Shochoh, and Azekah, in Ephesdammim. And Saul and the men of Israel were gathered together, and pitched by the valley of Elah, and set the battle in array against the Philistines. And the Philistines stood on a mountain on the one side, and Israel stood on a mountain on the other side: and there was a valley between them.

SYNOPSIS

The five lessons in this study on *How To Defeat the Giant You Are Facing* include:

- It's Time for You To Fight
- Stop Listening to the Giant You Are Facing
- It's Time To Get in the Fight
- Equipment Needed To Defeat Your Personal Giant
- Take the Head Off the Giant You Are Facing

The emphasis of this lesson:

Just like David, we all face times of conflict. In those moments, we can either stand on the sidelines trembling in fear, or we can accept the challenge as David did. When we step forward and fight in the name and power of the Lord, He'll give us victory as we trust Him.

The Valley of Elah is best known as the site of the great face-off between the Philistines and the army of Israel during the reign of King Saul. Located about 11 miles southwest of Jerusalem, Elah is situated between two mountains, and was once the stage upon which the Philistine champion Goliath experienced a crushing defeat by the supernatural power of

A Note From Rick Renner

I am on a personal quest to see a "revival of the Bible" so people can establish their lives on a firm foundation that will stand strong and endure the test as end-time storm winds begin to intensify.

In order to experience a revival of the Bible in your personal life, it is important to take time each day to read, receive, and apply its truths to your life. James tells us that if we will continue in the perfect law of liberty — refusing to be forgetful hearers, but determined to be doers — we will be blessed in our ways. As you watch or listen to the programs in this series and work through this corresponding study guide, I trust you will search the Scriptures and allow the Holy Spirit to help you hear something new from God's Word that applies specifically to your life. I encourage you to be a doer of the Word He reveals to you. Whatever the cost, I assure you — it will be worth it.

> Thy words were found, and I did eat them;
> and thy word was unto me the joy and rejoicing of mine heart:
> for I am called by thy name, O Lord God of hosts.
> — Jeremiah 15:16

Your brother and friend in Jesus Christ,

Rick Renner

How To Defeat the Giant You Are Facing

Copyright © 2019 by Rick Renner
1814 W. Tacoma St.
Broken Arrow, OK 74012-1406

Published by Rick Renner Ministries
www.renner.org

ISBN 13: 978-1-6803-1597-4

ISBN 13 eBook: 978-1-6803-1635-3

God. After 40 days of Israel's listening to their enemy's taunts, someone stepped forward into the battle zone to fight in the name of the God of Israel. That someone was David.

Who Were the Philistines?

Philistines were notoriously uncultured, uneducated, and uncivilized. They also had a reputation for being barbaric and warlike with everyone with which they had dealings.

Because the Philistines had no written language, the majority of historical data we have about them was written by other nations. Again and again, Philistines have been described as low-level, uncouth troublemakers and men of war. Even in some parts of the world today, some will occasionally call a person who's led by his base instincts a *Philistine.*

When it came to spirituality, the Philistines were pagans. Although they worshiped many gods, they primarily worshiped the fish god known as Dagon. This ruthless, warring culture of people caused trouble for all its neighbors and was greatly disliked. Indeed, the Philistines were sharp thorns in the side of Israel for centuries.

The Enemy Will Always Seize an Opportune Time

In First Samuel 17, the Bible says, "The Philistines gathered together their armies to battle, and were gathered together at Shochoh, which belongeth to Judah, and pitched between Shochoh, and Azekah, in Ephesdammim. And Saul and the men of Israel were gathered together, and pitched by the valley of Elah, and set the battle in array against the Philistines" (vv. 1, 2).

For many years there had been tension between these two nations. In fact, Israel had just scored a major victory against the Philistines under the leadership of King Saul and his son Jonathan (*see* 1 Samuel 14). After suffering great loss, the Philistines watched and waited for an opportune moment to take revenge, and it came just after God had rejected Saul for his disobedience regarding the Amalekites (*see* 1 Samuel 15:10-24).

When the blessing of God's favor had lifted from Saul, and Samuel vowed to never see him again, Saul slipped into a dark period of spiritual torment. He became very distracted by his own emotional instability.

Little by little, he dropped his guard and stopped paying attention to his enemies. The Philistines knew this and quickly moved in, gathering their army in Israel's territory.

That is how the enemy works. When we become complacent and let our guards down, the enemy comes in like a flood and attempts to establish a foothold in our lives from which he can strengthen and expand his influence. This is why the apostle Peter urged, "Be sober, be vigilant; because your adversary the devil, as a roaring lion, walketh about, seeking whom he may devour" (1 Peter 5:8). We can save ourselves much heartache by daily staying on guard against the devil's attacks

Why Did the Philistines Want the Valley of Elah?

The Valley of Elah was a cherished piece of real estate. It had historical and sentimental value and served as a major avenue of commerce, connecting the Mediterranean coastal region with the inland cities. It also provided access to a number of key towns nearby, including Bethlehem, the city of David; Hebron, the city of the patriarchs; and Jerusalem, which was about 16 miles away.

Elah was also about four miles from Ramah, the town where Samuel lived. This territory was very precious to the people of Israel as well as to King Saul personally; Samuel, who had played a major role in Saul's life, created many great memories for Saul in this region. Now those memories were under assault by Goliath and the Philistines.

Whoever controlled this strip of land controlled the whole region. The Philistines understood this, so while Saul was preoccupied with himself and how he looked in the eyes of his people, the Philistines rushed into Israel's territory and prepared for a fight: "And the Philistines stood on a mountain on the one side, and Israel stood on a mountain on the other side: and there was a valley between them" (1 Samuel 17:3).

Like Israel, We Must Be Prepared for Battle

The Bible says that Saul and the men of Israel "set the battle in array against the Philistines" (1 Samuel 17:2). The phrase "set the battle in array" is used 21 times in the Old Testament, and it means *to be fully weaponized and fit for battle*. The Philistines had infiltrated Judah's territory — the valley of Elah — and Israel was prepared and in position for a major conflict.

Just as Israel's armies were rallied to take up their position in battle, God wants you to take up your position and face your giant. He doesn't want you to shrink in fear or run and hide. He wants you to step forward and wage spiritual battle. Through the finished work of Jesus Christ, God has empowered you to defeat every attack Satan brings.

It is time for you to *set yourself in battle array* and deal with your situation. Wishing and hoping the enemy will just go away won't work. You must take action with the help of God to defend what belongs to you — to fell your giant and completely remove its influence from your life.

STUDY QUESTIONS

> Study to shew thyself approved unto God, a workman that needeth
> not to be ashamed, rightly dividing the word of truth.
> — 2 Timothy 2:15

1. You are a *winning warrior* in Christ Jesus! Meditate on the message of these amazing promises from the mouth of the Almighty: Romans 8:35, 37; Second Corinthians 2:14; and Luke 10:19. What do these verses personally say to you? Write out the one that most energizes your spirit.

2. Take a moment to read David's reaction to the threats of Goliath and about David's willingness to step forward and fight (*see* 1 Samuel 17:26, 32-37). What inspires you most from his conversation with King Saul? In what or whom did David anchor his confidence?

3. Rick gave several personal examples of times when he dropped his guard, and the enemy entered in and attacked. In what ways can you identify with what he experienced? What actions can you take to slay your own giant problems and challenges?

PRACTICAL APPLICATION

> But be ye doers of the word, and not hearers only,
> deceiving your own selves.
> — James 1:22

1. For David, the giant's name was Goliath. What is the name of the giant *you're* facing? Is it *physical sickness? Mental confusion? Financial lack? Problems in your marriage?* Briefly describe the menacing monster that has come against you.

2. Satan is constantly looking for an entrance into your life — a doorway through which he can legally enter and establish a foothold of influence and control. Pause and pray, "Lord, is there an area of my life where I have let my guard down? If so, where? What can I do to close the door and effectively defeat the enemy?" Be still and listen. What is the Holy Spirit showing you?

LESSON 2

TOPIC

Stop Listening to the Giant You Are Facing

SCRIPTURES

1. **1 Samuel 17:1-11** — Now the Philistines gathered together their armies to battle, and were gathered together at Shochoh, which belongeth to Judah, and pitched between Shochoh, and Azekah, in Ephesdammim. And Saul and the men of Israel were gathered together, and pitched by the valley of Elah, and set the battle in array against the Philistines. And the Philistines stood on a mountain on the one side, and Israel stood on a mountain on the other side: and there was a valley between them. And there went out a champion out of the camp of the Philistines, named Goliath, of Gath, whose height was six cubits and a span. And he had an helmet of brass upon his head, and he was armed with a coat of mail; and the weight of the coat was five thousand shekels of brass. And he had greaves of brass upon his legs, and a target of brass between his shoulders. And the staff of his spear was like a weaver's beam; and his spear's head weighed six hundred shekels of iron: and one bearing a shield went before him. And he stood and cried unto the armies of Israel, and said unto them, Why are ye come out to set your battle in array? Am not I a Philistine, and ye servants to Saul? choose you a man for you, and

let him come down to me. If he be able to fight with me, and to kill me, then will we be your servants: but if I prevail against him, and kill him, then shall ye be our servants, and serve us. And the Philistine said, I defy the armies of Israel this day; give me a man, that we may fight together. When Saul and all Israel heard those words of the Philistine, they were dismayed, and greatly afraid.

2. **1 Samuel 17:16** — And the Philistine drew near morning and evening, and presented himself forty days.

SYNOPSIS

In our first lesson, we learned about the Valley of Elah, located a few miles southwest of Jerusalem. It was there that Israel's forces once arrayed themselves for battle against the Philistines. Each army had positioned itself on a mountain directly across from the other, and the Valley of Elah lay between them. It was in this valley that Goliath, the Philistine champion, used his words to intimidate and immobilize God's people.

After King Saul and the people of Israel had scored a mighty victory against the Philistines, they dropped their guard and stopped paying attention to their enemies. The Philistines saw the opportunity and seized it, assembling their army in Elah in the territory of Judah. This was a precious place to Israel, filled with many fond memories of great victories and peace. Yet it was this valley that had become a place of conflict. First Samuel 17:3 says, "…The Philistines stood on a mountain on the one side, and Israel stood on a mountain on the other side: and there was a valley between them."

The emphasis of this lesson:

For 40 days, Goliath shouted threats and insults at Israel, effectively paralyzing them with fear. Satan tries to do the same thing in our lives. But if we're willing to seize God's power and turn a deaf ear to Satan's voice, God will enable us to defeat any giant and live in victory.

What Do We Know About Goliath?

First Samuel 17:4 says, "And there went out a champion out of the camp of the Philistines, named Goliath, of Gath, whose height was six cubits and a span." The word "champion" is a very old word, which seems to carry the meaning of *one that is born of unknown parents*. For this reason, some scholars have translated "champion" as "bastard," meaning *illegitimate child*.

Other scholars say the word "champion" means *one between two*, which indicates that Goliath was a champion negotiator — someone sent out to stand between enemies and resolve issues. That is what we find Goliath doing in First Samuel 17. His sheer size was so terrifying to behold that the Philistines used him to solve their problems with other nations.

The name "Goliath" means *to uncover or to reveal*. This indicates that when people took one look at him, it was quite a shocking *revelation*. He was an unknown character of mysterious origin, but who was too enormous in size to ignore.

The Bible says Goliath's height was "six cubits and a span." A cubit was eighteen to twenty-one inches in length, which means Goliath was anywhere from eight feet, nine inches, to nine feet, nine inches tall. Either way, his immense size clarifies why his name means *revelation*.

The 'Giant' Significance of Gath

The Bible says Goliath was from "Gath" — a community that was famous for a race of giants. Specifically, Gath was the home of the *Anakim*, the sons of Anak. These were the same giants that ten of the twelve spies noted were living in the Promised Land when they went to spy it out (*see* Numbers 13:28, 33).

A careful study of Scripture reveals that there were many races of giants on the earth — both before and after the flood (*see* Genesis 6:4). There was a legendary race of giants known as the *Rephaim* (*see* Deuteronomy 2:19-21), as well as giants who lived among the Kenites, Kenizzites, Hittites, Perizzites, Ammonites, Hivites, Jebusites, Girgashites, and Canaanites.

Again, Goliath was of the Anakim and was from the city of Gath. Interestingly, Second Samuel 21 tells of four other giants connected to Goliath. Verse 16 tells us about "…Ishbi-benob, which was of the sons of the giant, the weight of whose spear weighed three hundred shekels of brass…." Abishai killed him and protected David in the process.

In verse 18, we learn about "…Saph, which was of the sons of the giant," and in verse 19 we see the brother of Goliath, who had a staff "whose spear was like a weaver's beam." Then we come to verses 20 and 22, which say, "And there was yet a battle in Gath, where was a man of great stature, that had on every hand six fingers, and on every foot six toes, four and twenty in number; and he also was born to the giant.... These four were born to the giant in Gath, and fell by the hand of David, and by the hand of his servants."

Some scholars believe that the four giants mentioned in this chapter were four sons simply born to a giant. Other scholars believe these were specifically four sons of *Goliath*. In any case, there were five giants in all living in or very near the city of Gath. This explains why David selected five smooth stones from the brook in Elah and placed them in his shepherd's bag just before his fight with Goliath (*see* 1 Samuel 17:40). He knew that there were five giants he would potentially face. They were all related and would likely stand together. Thus, David took five stones — one stone for each giant.

The Mammoth Weight of Goliath's Armor

When Goliath walked onto the battlefield, he was well-armed. The Bible says, "He had an helmet of brass upon his head, and he was armed with a coat of mail; and the weight of the coat was five thousand shekels of brass" (1 Samuel 17:5). It is believed that Goliath's helmet weighed 15 pounds or more. And his coat of mail, which resembled the scales of a fish and covered his entire torso from shoulders to waist, front and back, weighed no less than 125 pounds.

"And he had greaves of brass upon his legs, and a target of brass between his shoulders" (1 Samuel 17:6). These "greaves of brass" were like brass boots. The Greeks and the Romans also wore greaves. Historically, each greave weighed twice the amount of the soldier's helmet. Therefore, if the helmet weighed 15 pounds, each brass boot (greave) weighed a minimum of 30 pounds. In other words, Goliath had at least 60 pounds of metal hammering the ground with every step he took.

Verse 7 says, "And the staff of his spear was like a weaver's beam; and his spear's head weighed six hundred shekels of iron: and one bearing a shield went before him." The staff of the spear describes the wooden portion of the spear, and Goliath's was 26 feet long and weighed in excess of 17 pounds. The spearhead itself weighed more than 37 pounds.

How about his shield? Although the weight and size are not listed, we know that it had to be enormous. In fact, it was so massive that Goliath employed another man to carry it and go before him when he went into battle.

Goliath also had a sword, which is not mentioned initially but is talked about later in Scripture. It was of the Hittite fashion and very unique. David would use the giant's own sword to cut off his head and ensure his defeat (*see* 1 Samuel 17:51). Goliath's sword later became a lifetime souvenir for David to remember his giant victory.

When you add the weight of all the pieces of Goliath's weaponry — the brass helmet, greaves, and coat of mail, plus the weight of his spear, sword, and shield — scholars estimate the total weight was somewhere between 500 and 700 pounds! Just imagine a nine- to ten-foot monster armed with 500 to 700 pounds of armor coming to kill you. Indeed, Goliath was a threatening menace.

Goliath's Words Carried the Greatest Weight

As frightening as his weapons were, it was Goliath's words that inflicted the heaviest damage on the army of Israel. First Samuel 17:8-11 says, "And he stood and cried unto the armies of Israel, and said unto them, Why are ye come out to set your battle in array? Am not I a Philistine, and ye servants to Saul? choose you a man for you, and let him come down to me. If he be able to fight with me, and to kill me, then will we be your servants: but if I prevail against him, and kill him, then shall ye be our servants, and serve us. And the Philistine said, I defy the armies of Israel this day; give me a man, that we may fight together. When Saul and all Israel heard those words of the Philistine, they were dismayed, and greatly afraid."

How long and how often did Goliath spew his threats and insults at the army of Israel? Verse 16 says, "The Philistine drew near morning and evening, and presented himself forty days." Again and again and again, Goliath defied the people of Israel, essentially saying, "Who do you think you are? Just try to fight me. You're no match for my superior skill. I'll defeat you and take you down!"

When Israel's soldiers heard Goliath's words, they were dismayed and greatly afraid — sapped of all courage to fight. The only one undaunted by the haunting words and immense size of the champion from Gath was a young shepherd boy named David.

David's life and tenacious faith in God clearly demonstrate that the Lord will use anyone who puts his trust in Him — regardless of his age, level of education, family pedigree, or financial status.

Is the enemy speaking words of fear and failure to you? Just stop listening to him! He is a liar and the father of lies. If you will shut your ears, and open your mouth to speak God's Word, the enemy will be driven out of your life.

STUDY QUESTIONS

> Study to shew thyself approved unto God, a workman that needeth not to be ashamed, rightly dividing the word of truth.
> — 2 Timothy 2:15

1. What new facts did you learn about Goliath and the giants living in the land of Israel?

2. According to Ephesians 6:13-18, what spiritual weaponry has God given you to withstand the enemy's attacks? Name the other devil-crushing weapon mentioned in Revelation 12:11 that Jesus Himself has provided? (Also consider Hebrews 9:14; 1 Peter 1:18, 19.)

PRACTICAL APPLICATION

> But be ye doers of the word, and not hearers only, deceiving your own selves.
> — James 1:22

1. The Bible says Goliath shouted the *same* insults and threats at Israel for 40 days. Stop and think: What fearful phrases and insults has the enemy repeatedly yelled in your ears?

2. What verses of Scripture come to mind that specifically contradict those intimidating words? (For help, use a Bible concordance to look up the key words that describe the cure for what you're facing.)

3. Many times the attacks of the enemy and your reactions to them have a *pattern*. Take a few moments to reflect on previous conflicts. What lessons can you learn from them and apply in the present to keep you from having to face the same kinds of giants again and again?

TOPIC

It's Time To Get in the Fight

SCRIPTURES

1. **1 Samuel 17:11-26** — When Saul and all Israel heard those words
    of the Philistine, they were dismayed, and greatly afraid. Now David
    was the son of that Ephrathite of Bethlehemjudah, whose name was
    Jesse; and he had eight sons: and the man went among men for an old
    man in the days of Saul. And the three eldest sons of Jesse went and
    followed Saul to the battle: and the names of his three sons that went
    to the battle were Eliab the firstborn, and next unto him Abinadab,
    and the third Shammah. And David was the youngest: and the three
    eldest followed Saul. But David went and returned from Saul to feed
    his father's sheep at Bethlehem. And the Philistine drew near morn-
    ing and evening, and presented himself forty days. And Jesse said unto
    David his son, Take now for thy brethren an ephah of this parched
    corn, and these ten loaves, and run to the camp to thy brethren and
    carry these ten cheeses unto the captain of their thousand, and look
    how thy brethren fare, and take their pledge. Now Saul, and they [the
    three elder brothers], and all the men of Israel, were in the valley of
    Elah, fighting with the Philistines. And David rose up early in the
    morning, and left the sheep with a keeper, and took, and went, as
    Jesse had commanded him; and he came to the trench, as the host
    was going forth to the fight, and shouted for the battle. For Israel
    and the Philistines had put the battle in array, army against army.
    And David left his carriage in the hand of the keeper of the carriage,
    and ran into the army, and came and saluted his brethren. And as he
    talked with them, behold, there came up the champion, the Philistine
    of Gath, Goliath by name, out of the armies of the Philistines, and
    spake according to the same words: and David heard them. And all
    the men of Israel, when they saw the man, fled from him, and were
    sore afraid. And the men of Israel said, Have ye seen this man that is
    come up? surely to defy Israel is he come up: and it shall be, that the
    man who killeth him, the king will enrich him with great riches, and
    will give him his daughter, and make his father's house free in Israel.

And David spake to the men that stood by him, saying, What shall be done to the man that killeth this Philistine, and taketh away the reproach from Israel? for who is this uncircumcised Philistine, that he should defy the armies of the living God?

2. **1 Samuel 17:28-32** — And Eliab his eldest brother heard when he spake unto the men; and Eliab's anger was kindled against David, and he said, Why camest thou down hither? and with whom hast thou left those few sheep in the wilderness? I know thy pride, and the naughtiness of thine heart; for thou art come down that thou mightest see the battle. And David said, What have I now done? Is there not a cause? And he turned from him toward another, and spake after the same manner: And the people answered him again after the former manner. And when the words were heard which David spake, they rehearsed them before Saul: and he sent for him. And David said to Saul, Let no man's heart fail because of him; thy servant will go and fight with this Philistine.

3. **1 Samuel 16:18** — Then answered one of the servants, and said, Behold, I have seen a son of Jesse the Bethlehemite, that is cunning in playing, and a mighty valiant man, and a man of war, and prudent in matters, and a comely person, and the Lord is with him.

SYNOPSIS

Goliath was a menacing monster to behold. His immense size, along with the 500 to 700 pounds of weaponry he carried, was quite intimidating. Day after day, every morning and evening, he ventured down into the valley of Elah, defiantly shouting threats and insults against Israel and the Lord their God.

First Samuel 17:11 says, "When Saul and all Israel heard those words of the Philistine, they were dismayed, and greatly afraid." Verse 24 tells us, "All the men of Israel, when they saw the man, fled from him, and were sore afraid." For 40 days, Israel's army remained frozen, fearful of the overwhelming presence of the Philistine champion. Only the faith and fearlessness of David could defeat the giant and bring victory to Israel.

The emphasis of this lesson:

The armies of Israel focused on Goliath's immense size, his weaponry, and his words, and they became paralyzed by fear. David, in contrast, focused on God's greatness and thus was able to remain in faith and get

into the fight. When you follow David's example, you, too, can wage war against the enemy and win.

What Does the Bible Say About David?

First Samuel 17:12 tells us, "David was the son of that Ephrathite of Bethlehemjudah, whose name was Jesse; and he had eight sons...." The word "son" here indicates that David was a very young man — perhaps young enough to still be going through puberty.

When we turn back to First Samuel 16:18, we get a detailed description of who David was. When King Saul had asked for a man who could play the harp well, one of his servants responded, "...Behold, I have seen a son of Jesse the Bethlehemite, that is cunning in playing, and a mighty valiant man, and a man of war, and prudent in matters, and a comely person, and the Lord is with him." This verse gives us six characteristics of David.

First, David was "cunning in playing." This means he had a desire to become the best musician possible. When he was all alone taking care of his father's sheep, and no one could hear him except God and the animals he watched over, David practiced his instrument until he played like a professional. He never knew he would write songs that would be sung in palaces and places across the globe for centuries after he was gone. He simply had a desire to develop his gift.

Second, David was "a mighty valiant man." This indicates that he was willing to stand and fight, regardless of the odds that were against him. As a young shepherd boy, he delivered his father's sheep from the attacks of a lion and a bear. He took his responsibilities seriously — even when his own life was at risk.

Third, David was "a man of war." Essentially, this means he was a man of principle; he would not budge from his convictions or surrender territory that was under his keeping. He was determined and committed to stand for and to do what was right.

Fourth, David was "prudent in matters." This phrase specifically refers to his excellent business skills. Although David was the youngest of eight sons, his father Jesse had placed him in charge over the family business. In those days, sheep were big business. The more a person had, the richer he was. Obviously, Jesse trusted David greatly to give him oversight of his flocks.

Fifth, David was "a comely person." The fact that David was "a comely person" meant he cared about the way he looked. With great discipline, he groomed himself and maintained his personal appearance.

The **sixth** and most important feature of David's life was that "the Lord was with him." This means he had a spiritual life. He was anointed by God because he was connected with God. In fact, the Lord was so aware of David's devotion that God anointed and appointed him to take Saul's place as the next king of Israel while David was still a very young man.

David Was Sent to His Three Siblings at the Frontline

Returning to our story in First Samuel 17, the Bible says, "The three eldest sons of Jesse went and followed Saul to the battle: and the names of his three sons that went to the battle were Eliab the firstborn, and next unto him Abinadab, and the third Shammah. And David was the youngest: and the three eldest followed Saul. But David went and returned from Saul to feed his father's sheep at Bethlehem" (vv. 13-15). Verses 17-19 then continue with why David went to the battlefield:

> And Jesse said unto David his son, Take now for thy brethren an ephah of this parched corn, and these ten loaves, and run to the camp to thy brethren; and carry these ten cheeses unto the captain of their thousand, and look how thy brethren fare, and take their pledge. Now Saul, and they [the three elder brothers], and all the men of Israel, were in the valley of Elah, fighting with the Philistines.

Remember, the Valley of Elah was a prized piece of land. It was a very strategic location, connecting the coastal lands to a number of inland cities, such as Bethlehem, Hebron, and Jerusalem. It was also about four miles from historic Ramah where the prophet Samuel once lived. This precious patch of real estate was now under siege, and the men of Israel had stepped forward to fight and maintain possession of it.

First Samuel 17:20-22 goes on to say, "David rose up early in the morning, and left the sheep with a keeper, and took, and went, as Jesse had commanded him; and he came to the trench, as the host was going forth to the fight, and shouted for the battle. For Israel and the Philistines had put the battle in array, army against army. And David left his carriage in the hand of the keeper of the carriage, and ran into the army, and came and saluted his brethren."

Once David arrived at the frontline, he saw the giant and heard the taunts of the Philistine champion. The Bible says the giant "…spake according to the same words: and David heard them" (1 Samuel 17:23). What "same words" did David hear? The same threats and insults against God and Israel that Goliath had been speaking the previous 40 days (*see* 1 Samuel 17:8-10).

The Great Reward for Defeating the Giant

As Goliath uttered his intimidating verbal abuse, King Saul and the army of Israel hid in fear. David, on the other hand, became infuriated at the giant's blasphemies. The Scripture states, "The men of Israel said, Have ye seen this man that is come up? surely to defy Israel is he come up: and it shall be, that the man who killeth him, the king will enrich him with great riches, and will give him his daughter, and make his father's house free in Israel" (1 Samuel 17:25).

When David first heard the details of the reward, he couldn't believe what he was hearing. *Did I hear that correctly?* he thought. Immediately, he turned to the men standing beside him and asked, "…What shall be done to the man that killeth this Philistine, and taketh away the reproach from Israel?" (1 Samuel 17:26). Once again, the same particulars of the reward were articulated: To the one who defeated the giant, the king would give great riches, his daughter's hand in marriage, and a tax-exempt status for life.

At that point, Eliab became angry and accused his youngest brother, saying, "…Why camest thou down hither? and with whom hast thou left those few sheep in the wilderness? I know thy pride, and the naughtiness of thine heart; for thou art come down that thou mightest see the battle" (1 Samuel 17:28).

Upon receiving this tremendous insult, David replied, "…What have I now done? Is there not a cause?" (1 Samuel 17:29). By asking his second question, David was saying, in effect, "Isn't there a reason to stand up and fight for what is right? Is not the reputation of the God of Israel worth defending? This uncircumcised Philistine has blasphemed the name of the Lord, and if no one else is going to do anything, I'm going to take care of it."

Words of Faith Will Propel You to Inconceivable Places

The Bible says, "And when the words were heard which David spake, they rehearsed them before Saul: and he sent for him. And David said to Saul, Let no man's heart fail because of him; thy servant will go and fight with this Philistine" (1 Samuel 17:31, 32).

Like David, when you stand and speak words of faith, it will capture people's attention — including people in high places. King Saul was desperately looking for someone who was bold and brave and willing to stand against the giant. When he heard what David had said, David's fearlessness and faith made way for him and brought him before the king.

Israel's mistake was focusing on Goliath instead of on God's greatness. As a result, they were filled with fear and emptied of power. David, on the other hand, demonstrates what happens when we focus on the power of God and not on the problems in front of us.

Friend, your faith will take you to places you could never imagine. If you will run to the battle, trusting God for His power, you will win the victory and take home the prize.

STUDY QUESTIONS

Study to shew thyself approved unto God, a workman that needeth not to be ashamed, rightly dividing the word of truth.
— 2 Timothy 2:15

1. One characteristic that marked the life of David was that the Lord was with him. According to his words in Psalm 27:4-9, how important was the Lord's presence to David?

2. Consider the value Moses placed on the presence of God in Exodus 33:12-17. Ask yourself this question: *Just how important and valuable is the presence of God to me?*

3. The army of Israel was focused on Goliath, and as a result, they were filled with fear and emptied of power. What does God's Word tell us to focus on in Hebrews 12:2; Psalm 34:4, 5; 123:1, 2; and 141:8-10? What can you expect to happen when you obey these instructions?

PRACTICAL APPLICATION

But be ye doers of the word, and not hearers only,
deceiving your own selves.
—James 1:22

At the opening of this lesson, Rick shared a personal story of how the devil attacked his mind when he was young, telling him repeatedly that he was *stupid.* Satan then used a school teacher and a guidance counselor to repeat and reinforce this lie in Rick's mind. But when he was filled with the Holy Spirit, God's power moved in, exposing and eradicating that lie from his life.

1. What lie has the devil repeatedly fed your mind, maybe even ever since you were a child?
2. How has he used the voices of others to reinforce his negative statements?
3. What truths can you find in God's Word that refute this lie and speak life to your spirit?

LESSON 4

TOPIC
Equipment Needed To Defeat Your Personal Giant

SCRIPTURES

1. **1 Samuel 17:31-40** — And when the words were heard which David spake, they rehearsed them before Saul: and he sent for him. And David said to Saul, Let no man's heart fail because of him; thy servant will go and fight with this Philistine. And Saul said to David, Thou art not able to go against this Philistine to fight with him: for thou art but a youth, and he a man of war from his youth. And David said unto Saul, Thy servant kept his father's sheep, and there came a lion, and a bear, and took a lamb out of the flock. And I went out after him, and smote him, and delivered it out of his mouth: and when he arose against me, I caught him by his beard, and smote him, and slew him.

Thy servant slew both the lion and the bear: and this uncircumcised Philistine shall be as one of them, seeing he hath defied the armies of the living God. David said moreover, The Lord that delivered me out of the paw of the lion, and out of the paw of the bear, he will deliver me out of the hand of this Philistine. And Saul said unto David, Go, and the Lord be with thee. And Saul armed David with his armour, and he put an helmet of brass upon his head; also he armed him with a coat of mail. And David girded his sword upon his armour, and he assayed to go; for he had not proved it. And David said unto Saul, I cannot go with these; for I have not proved them. And David put them off him. And he took his staff in his hand, and chose him five smooth stones out of the brook, and put them in a shepherd's bag which he had, even in a scrip; and his sling was in his hand: and he drew near to the Philistine.

SYNOPSIS

The account of David and Goliath is a favorite for many people, and it's important to realize that it is not a fairytale; it is an actual event that took place about 3,000 years ago in the Valley of Elah. There really was a Philistine giant named Goliath and a young shepherd boy named David. When King Saul and the army of Israel had lost heart by focusing on the enemy, David grew strong in faith as he focused on God's greatness. He had experienced the Lord's supernatural delivering power in the past and was trusting Him to do it again.

The emphasis of this lesson:

Just as David was fully equipped to defeat Goliath, you have everything you need to defeat the giant in your life.

Faith-Filled Words Brought David Before the King

Just after David arrived at the frontline of the battle in Elah, he saw Goliath and heard firsthand the threats and insults the giant had been voicing for 40 days. The men of Israel then informed David of the huge reward being offered by King Saul to the man who killed the giant: *great riches, the king's daughter for his wife,* and *tax-free status for life.*

Although this reward was highly desired by David, he was also a man of principle who believed in standing up and fighting for what was right. To hear the Philistine champion ridicule and blaspheme the name of the Lord and the people of Israel again and again was wrong, and somebody needed to take action against him.

"Who is this uncircumcised Philistine, that he should defy the armies of the living God?" David cried. "Is there not a cause?" (1 Samuel 17:26, 29). Essentially, David was saying, "Is there not a reason to stand up and do something about this giant? Aren't God's reputation and the nation of Israel worth defending? This uncircumcised Philistine has blasphemed the name of the Lord, and if no one else is going to do anything about it, I will!"

"And when the words were heard which David spake, they rehearsed them before Saul: and he sent for him" (1 Samuel 17:31). This demonstrates that when you speak faith-filled words, it gets people's attention. David's bold declarations brought him before the king. "And David said to Saul, Let no man's heart fail because of him; thy servant will go and fight with this Philistine" (1 Samuel 17:32).

David Had a Testimony That He Was Leaning On

Immediately after David declared he would go and fight Goliath, "Saul said to David, Thou art not able to go against this Philistine to fight with him: for thou art but a youth, and he a man of war from his youth" (1 Samuel 17:33). This was the equivalent of Saul saying, "You're not old enough. You have no experience. You've never fought on the frontlines with a skilled warrior like Goliath. He's a professional killer; you're an inexperienced 'wannabe.'"

Saul was a naysayer, and when *you* hear negative words from naysayers about what you can't do, you need to do as David did. David politely dismissed Saul's pessimism by declaring God's track record of past victories in his life. Listen to his words of courage and faith in First Samuel 17:34-37:

And David said unto Saul, Thy servant kept his father's sheep, and there came a lion, and a bear, and took a lamb out of the flock. And I went out after him, and smote him, and delivered it out of his mouth: and when he arose against me, I caught him by his beard, and smote him, and slew him. Thy servant slew both the lion and the bear: and this uncircumcised Philistine shall be as one of them, seeing he hath defied the armies of the living God. David said moreover, The Lord that delivered me out of the paw of the lion, and out of the paw of the bear, he will deliver me out of the hand of this Philistine.

David had a testimony of God's faithful deliverance in extremely difficult situations. Infused with God's strength, David had already done the impossible. Thus, the seemingly impossible matchup against Goliath was just one more opportunity for God to show Himself strong on David's behalf.

You, too, have a testimony. There are things God has already done in and through your life that no one on earth can argue or explain away. Instead of listening to the enemy's terrorizing threats or mulling over thoughts of doubt and unbelief, lean on the testimony of God's faithfulness. It is a firm foundation on which to stand. That's what David did, and it served him well.

How You See Your 'Giant' Is Critical

The way we view the "giants" in our lives determines whether we defeat them or they immobilize and defeat us. The men of Israel were *looking* at Goliath's size, *listening* to his words, and *focusing* on his powerful weaponry. With each passing day, when the giant presented himself, he became bigger and bigger in their eyes. The way they viewed Goliath caused them to be paralyzed in with fear.

David, on the other hand, viewed Goliath as an "uncircumcised Philistine." Basically, David saw him and said, "This giant is just another common lowlife like all the other blasphemers against God. I can handle him with no problem." He minimized the giant instead of magnifying him.

First Corinthians 10:13 communicates this principle. It says, "There hath no temptation taken you but such as is common to man...." In the Greek, the phrase "common to man" describes *things that are normally experienced by human beings* or *something minimal, common, or ordinary.*

If you view your trial, your temptation, or whatever you're facing as uncommon and larger than life, it will become more and more magnified in your mind and much harder to overcome. However, if you view what you're going through as *minimal, common,* or *ordinary,* its size will become smaller and smaller in your mind, making it much easier to overcome.

David told King Saul, "The Lord has delivered me out of the paw of the lion and the paw of the bear, and He will deliver me from the hand of this lowlife Philistine." When Saul heard these words spoken with such confidence and faith in God, he said to David, "Go, and the Lord be with thee."

Wearing the Armor of Others Will Not Work

After David received the go-ahead from King Saul, Saul tried to equip David with *his* weaponry. The Bible says, "Saul armed David with his armour, and he put an helmet of brass upon his head; also he armed him with a coat of mail. And David girded his sword upon his armour, and he assayed to go; for he had not proved it…" (1 Samuel 17:38, 39).

Can you imagine what David looked like? Saul, who was quite tall (*see* 1 Samuel 10:23), put his extra-large armor on young David — a young shepherd boy. One could imagine the helmet swallowing his head; the coat of mail coming down below his knees; and the sword swinging as long as his legs. No doubt it was wonderful weaponry for King Saul, but it was probably grossly oversized for David.

It is important to note that David didn't rebuff or rebuke Saul for dressing him in his armor. Instead, he respectfully cooperated with him and tried to receive his help. But when none of his weaponry looked right, fit right, or felt right, "…David said unto Saul, I cannot go with these; for I have not proved them. And David put them off him" (1 Samuel 17:39).

Realize that when you step out and begin to do something for God, well-meaning people will often tell you how to do it. Some will give you advice on the schooling you need, and others will tell you the specific steps you need to take — steps that they themselves walked out to accomplish things for God.

It is fine to respectfully listen, and sometimes their advice *will* help you fulfill your dream or conquer your enemy. Nevertheless, if you try to do what they've suggested and it doesn't work, set it aside. "Thank you for wanting to help me," you can say, "but I believe God wants me to do things another way." Always remember your aim and obligation is to please God, not people.

Use Weapons With Which You Have Experience

Once David took off Saul's armor, he turned to weaponry with which he had experience. First Samuel 17:40 says, "And he took his staff in his hand, and chose him five smooth stones out of the brook, and put them in a shepherd's bag which he had, even in a scrip; and his sling was in his hand: and he drew near to the Philistine." David grabbed hold of what he knew how to use. He moved forward to the fight with what he had experience with because it empowered him.

First, we see that he took his *staff* in his hand. This was a large cane that he had used on many occasions to direct and correct his sheep. He grabbed his staff because he knew that if he needed to, he could beat the giant to death with it. He was that committed to experiencing victory over his enemy.

Also notice that David picked up *five smooth stones* from the brook that ran through the Valley of Elah to use in his sling. Remember, in one of our previous lessons, we learned that Goliath wasn't the only giant in the region. There were four others, and they were all related (*see* 2 Samuel 21:16-22). David was aware that there were five giants in all, so he took one stone for every giant, just in case they all showed up. He was confident in the power of God and his ability to use the weapons with which he had experience.

Thus with his staff in hand, five smooth stones, and his sling, David drew near to the Philistine champion. Yet, he didn't move with natural equipment alone — he moved with supernatural equipment. He was leaning on his previous experiences of trusting God. That is what made him fit for battle.

Friend, God has given you all the supernatural equipment and weaponry you need to defeat the giants in your life! He's provided the blood of Jesus, the name of Jesus, His Holy Spirit, and His Holy Word. It's time to stand up and move forward toward the giant you've been facing. Victory awaits!

STUDY QUESTIONS

Study to shew thyself approved unto God, a workman that needeth
not to be ashamed, rightly dividing the word of truth.
— 2 Timothy 2:15

1. The Lord equipped David to defeat Goliath, and He has equipped
you to defeat every attack the enemy brings your way. Write out the
two amazing promises God has made to you in Ephesians 1:3 and
Second Peter 1:3, and take time to meditate on them.

2. Initially, David was wearing Saul's armor, but he quickly realized he
couldn't step out and fight in armor that was made for someone else.
Are you trying to fight while wearing someone else's "armor"? If it
doesn't look right, fit right, or feel right, you need to take it off. What
weaponry can you put on with which you already have experience?

PRACTICAL APPLICATION

But be ye doers of the word, and not hearers only,
deceiving your own selves.
— James 1:22

1. Revelation 12:11 says that we overcome Satan by the blood of the
Lamb and the word of our testimony. Stop and think: *What is the
word of my testimony?* What are some of the impossible things you
know that God has done in and through your life? These are part of
your testimony, and you can confidently lean on it for strength.

2. How you see your "giant" is crucial. The men of Israel were *looking*
at Goliath's size, *listening* to his words, and *focusing* on his powerful
weaponry. With each passing day, he became bigger and bigger in
their eyes. David, on the other hand, saw Goliath as *minimal, common,*
and *ordinary.* Who would you say you are more like — David or the
men of Israel?

3. Looking at the landscape of your life, what giants (problems, trials,
temptations, challenges) do you need the help of the Holy Spirit to
see differently? Take time right now to pray and invite Him into your
life and situation.

TOPIC

Take the Head Off the Giant You Are Facing

SCRIPTURES

1. **1 Samuel 17:37** — David said moreover, The Lord that delivered me out of the paw of the lion, and out of the paw of the bear, he will deliver me out of the hand of this Philistine. And Saul said unto David, Go, and the Lord be with thee.

2. **1 Samuel 17:40-54, 57, 58** — And he took his staff in his hand, and chose him five smooth stones out of the brook, and put them in a shepherd's bag which he had, even in a scrip; and his sling was in his hand: and he drew near to the Philistine. And the Philistine came on and drew near unto David; and the man that bare the shield went before him. And when the Philistine looked about, and saw David, he disdained him: for he was but a youth, and ruddy, and of a fair countenance. And the Philistine said unto David, Am I a dog, that thou comest to me with staves? And the Philistine cursed David by his gods. And the Philistine said to David, Come to me, and I will give thy flesh unto the fowls of the air, and to the beasts of the field. Then said David to the Philistine, Thou comest to me with a sword, and with a spear, and with a shield: but I come to thee in the name of the Lord of hosts, the God of the armies of Israel, whom thou hast defied. This day will the Lord deliver thee into mine hand; and I will smite thee, and take thine head from thee; and I will give the carcases of the host of the Philistines this day unto the fowls of the air, and to the wild beasts of the earth; that all the earth may know that there is a God in Israel. And all this assembly shall know that the Lord saveth not with sword and spear: for the battle is the Lord's, and he will give you into our hands. And it came to pass, when the Philistine arose, and came and drew nigh to meet David, that David hasted, and ran toward the army to meet the Philistine. And David put his hand in his bag, and took thence a stone, and slang it, and smote the Philistine in his forehead, that the stone sunk into his forehead; and he

fell upon his face to the earth. So David prevailed over the Philistine with a sling and with a stone, and smote the Philistine, and slew him; but there was no sword in the hand of David. Therefore David ran, and stood upon the Philistine, and took his sword, and drew it out of the sheath thereof, and slew him, and cut off his head therewith. And when the Philistines saw their champion was dead, they fled. And the men of Israel and of Judah arose, and shouted, and pursued the Philistines, until thou come to the valley, and to the gates of Ekron. And the wounded of the Philistines fell down by the way to Shaaraim, even unto Gath, and unto Ekron. And the children of Israel returned from chasing after the Philistines, and they spoiled their tents. And David took the head of the Philistine, and brought it to Jerusalem; but he put his armour in his tent. And as David returned from the slaughter of the Philistine, Abner took him, and brought him before Saul with the head of the Philistine in his hand. And Saul said to him, Whose son art thou, thou young man? And David answered, I am the son of thy servant Jesse the Bethlehemite.

SYNOPSIS

As fear gripped the hearts of the men of Israel, words of faith flowed freely from the lips of David. This shepherd boy from Bethlehem — armed with only his staff, his sling, and five smooth stones — put on display the unprecedented power of Jehovah. By faith, he partnered with the power of God and obtained a great victory over Goliath, the Philistine champion. With a release of his sling and a swing of the giant's sword, David made history, and it all took place in the valley of Elah.

The emphasis of this lesson:

The fight David faced against Goliath seemed impossible to win. Yet he confessed in faith the victory he knew was possible. With a sling and a stone, he brought down his enemy, finishing him off with the giant's own sword. As you trust God and act in faith, your giants will also be defeated.

David Was Fully Equipped To Win

As we concluded our last lesson, we saw how King Saul dressed David in armor that didn't fit him or feel right. After David respectfully declined the use of Saul's equipment, he reached for the weaponry with which he had experience: his staff, his sling, and five smooth stones (*see* 1 Samuel 17:40). With confidence in the Lord who had given him victory before, David drew near to the Philistine.

Why the staff? David had used the shepherd's staff many times to direct and correct his sheep. If for some reason the sling and the stones didn't work, David was ready to take his staff and beat the giant to death. He was that determined to have victory.

Why the five stones? As we discovered in the previous two lessons, Goliath wasn't the only giant. Second Samuel 21:16-22 reveals that there were four other giants living in or very near the city of Gath. They were either Goliath's four sons or his four brothers. In either case, these five giants were all related, and David knew that. Therefore, he took one stone for each giant and was prepared to take out not just one, but all of the giants if necessary!

David was highly proficient with his weaponry. In the natural, he looked like he was no match for Goliath. The giant towered in height and was equipped with 500 to 700 pounds of armor. Nevertheless, David knew how to use his staff, his sling, and the stones. He had experience. More importantly, he had all the power of God backing him. That same power is available to you.

Goliath's Reaction Is a Picture of the Devil's Interaction With You

As David stepped onto the battlefield, the Bible says, "The Philistine came on and drew near unto David; and the man that bare the shield went before him" (1 Samuel 17:41). This means David wasn't just facing one opponent; he was facing *two* — Goliath and his shield bearer. But David wasn't alone; God was with him. And God plus anyone always equals a majority.

First Samuel 17:42 says, "And when the Philistine looked about, and saw David, he disdained him: for he was but a youth, and ruddy, and of a fair countenance." The word "saw" carries the idea of great *shock*. Goliath had been calling out every morning and evening for a man to come and fight him, and a boy showed up instead. When he "saw" David, he was shocked and "he disdained him," which means Goliath *mocked* David — he *laughed at him, ridiculed him, and insulted him.*

Goliath's response to David is a picture of how the devil responds to you when you stand your ground against him. He mocks you — he laughs at you, ridicules you, and shouts his insults. "Who do you think you are?" he snarls. "You are no match for me! You're a weak, powerless, fool to think you can defeat me." Essentially, that was Goliath's response to David. He was trying to drive him out of the valley, but David wouldn't budge. He was committed to victory.

When the Bible says David "was but a youth, and ruddy, and of a fair countenance," it means that when compared to the men of war who were fighting, he was very *young*. The word "ruddy" refers to his *complexion*. If David was still going through puberty, as we saw in Lesson 3, it would have been evident in his face. This verse also says he had a "fair countenance" (1 Samuel 17:42), which indicates he looked like a beautiful young boy, not a man.

"And the Philistine said unto David, Am I a dog, that thou comest to me with staves? And the Philistine cursed David by his gods" (1 Samuel 17:43). The word "staves" refers to David's *shepherd's staff*. Then, after insulting David, the giant began to provoke and incite him, saying, "... Come to me, and I will give thy flesh unto the fowls of the air, and to the beasts of the field" (1 Samuel 17:44).

Again, Goliath's taunts are a picture of what the devil says to you. "Just try to stand against me," he growls. "You're not going to make it. You're going to fall flat on your face and fail. Then I'm going to eat you alive." David heard but ignored the giant's threats, and they came to naught. The same holds true for you. When the devil speaks, turn a deaf ear to his lies and hold tightly in faith to God's Word.

David Responded by Declaring Five Confessions of Faith

Apparently, once Goliath verbally assaulted David and the God of Israel, he lay down (this is confirmed in verse 48). By doing this, the giant showed that he was unimpressed by David and was basically ignoring him. "Then said David to the Philistine, Thou comest to me with a sword, and with a spear, and with a shield: but I come to thee in the name of the Lord of hosts, the God of the armies of Israel, whom thou hast defied" (1 Samuel 17:45).

David's words reveal what his faith and confidence were anchored in — the name of the Lord of hosts, the God of the armies of Israel. Similarly, just as David came in the name of the Lord, you are to come against your giants in the name of Jesus. In His name, you have all power and all authority over the enemy (*see* Luke 10:19).

After this exchange of words, David made five confessions of faith in the hearing of Goliath and all who were present. These declarations are all found in First Samuel 17:46 and 47:

1. "This day will the Lord deliver thee into mine hand."
2. "I will smite thee."
3. "I will take thine head from thee."
4. "I will give the carcases of the host of the Philistines this day unto the fowls of the air, and to the wild beasts of the earth."
5. "The Lord will give you into our hands."

With great confidence in the Lord, David made these five confessions of faith. Even though Goliath was lying down in utter contempt, David boldly declared his intentions anyway. In the same way, God wants you to proclaim your faith regardless of who's listening or not listening.

David Ran *Toward* the Enemy

First Samuel 17:48 says, "And it came to pass, when the Philistine arose, and came and drew nigh to meet David, that David hasted, and ran toward the army to meet the Philistine." Three times the Bible emphasizes that David "hastened" or "ran" toward the enemy, which is important. He didn't wait for Goliath to come to him; *he charged the giant.* He was focused, determined, and serious about defeating his enemy. Likewise, God wants you to go after whatever is threatening you and not to shrink back in fear.

> And David put his hand in his bag, and took thence a stone, and slang it, and smote the Philistine in his forehead, that the stone sunk into his forehead; and he fell upon his face to the earth. So David prevailed over the Philistine with a sling and with a stone, and smote the Philistine, and slew him; but there was no sword in the hand of David.
>
> 1 Samuel 17:49, 50

It's important to see that the stone only stunned the giant and knocked him to the ground; it didn't kill him. The job wasn't finished. "Therefore David ran, and stood upon the Philistine, and took his sword, and drew it out of the sheath thereof, and slew him, and cut off his head therewith. And when the Philistines saw their champion was dead, they fled" (1 Samuel 17:51).

Goliath was killed with his own weapon. The very sword the giant had intended to use to destroy David, David used to destroy the giant. This is an established principle found throughout the books of Psalms and Proverbs: Our enemies will be destroyed by their own devices — the very weapons they intend to use against us will be turned against them!

Faith Ignites Faith in Others

Once David killed Goliath, notice the response of the men of Israel and Judah. Verses 52 and 53 tell us, "The men of Israel and of Judah arose, and shouted, and pursued the Philistines, until thou come to the valley, and to the gates of Ekron. And the wounded of the Philistines fell down by the way to Shaaraim, even unto Gath, and unto Ekron. And the children of Israel returned from chasing after the Philistines, and they spoiled their tents."

Once David's feats of faith produced victory, faith was ignited in the people. This reveals that when others see victorious faith in action, they throw off fear and unbelief and begin to act in faith themselves. They just need an example of someone to lead the way.

The truth is, people are watching you. When they see you take a step of faith and charge the enemy or overcome difficult circumstances, you encourage them to do the same. One victory leads to another victory. Remember that it is never all about you. Scripture says, "He who heeds instruction and correction is [not only himself] in the way of life [but also] *is a way of life for others…*" (Proverbs 10:17 *AMPC*).

Hold On to Your Souvenirs of Victory

What did David do once he decapitated Goliath? First Samuel 17:54 says, "David took the head of the Philistine, and brought it to Jerusalem; but he put his armour in his tent." Immediately after his triumph, David took Goliath's armor and put it in his tent, but he carried Goliath's head around as a souvenir of victory for quite some time — eventually taking it to Jerusalem.

Verse 57 states, "As David returned from the slaughter of the Philistine, Abner took him, and brought him before Saul with the head of the Philistine in his hand." The giant's head was David's souvenir. Every time the young shepherd boy was tempted to doubt God's greatness or his ability to tackle what was in front of him, David would look at that head. It was a visible reminder of the Lord's faithfulness in the midst of seemingly impossible situations.

As David stood before the king with the head of Goliath still firmly in his grasp, "Saul said to him, Whose son art thou, thou young man? And David answered, I am the son of thy servant Jesse the Bethlehemite" (1 Samuel 17:58). When he could have taken all of the glory for himself, he didn't. Instead, David honored his father before the king, announcing his identity by name.

Do you have any souvenirs of victory in your life? You need to remember them and carry those memories with you wherever you go. They are visible reminders that God will once again help you defeat the present giant you are facing.

STUDY QUESTIONS

Study to shew thyself approved unto God, a workman that needeth not to be ashamed, rightly dividing the word of truth.
— 2 Timothy 2:15

1. The principle that the enemy will be destroyed by his own devices is found throughout God's Word — including Psalm 9:15; Proverbs 26:27; 28:10; and Ecclesiastes 10:8. Carefully read these verses and jot down what the Holy Spirit speaks to you.

2. Does it seem like evil people do their wicked deeds and get away with them? That's how it appeared to David at one point, but God spoke to him and revealed the truth. Read what David learned about the outcome awaiting the wicked in Psalm 37:1-16. What facts are repeatedly mentioned in these verses, and what's your greatest takeaway?

PRACTICAL APPLICATION

But be ye doers of the word, and not hearers only,
deceiving your own selves.
—James 1:22

1. Do you have any *souvenirs of victory* in your life — tangible or intangible keepsakes of times when you trusted God, and He gave you success? If so, describe one or two of these souvenirs and explain what they remind you of?

2. As David stood before Goliath, he voiced five confessions of faith that all came true. In light of your present challenging situation, what declarations of faith do you feel prompted to make? If you're not sure, pray and ask the Holy Spirit for His wisdom and the words to speak. (Write down your confessions so that when they come true, you can look back on them and thank God for His faithfulness.)

A Prayer To Receive Salvation

If you've never received Jesus as your Savior and Lord, now is the time for you to experience the new life Jesus wants to give you! To receive God's gift of salvation that can be obtained through Jesus alone, pray this prayer from your heart:

Jesus, I repent of my sin and receive You as my Savior and Lord. Wash away my sin with Your precious blood and make me completely new. I thank You that my sin is removed, and Satan no longer has any right to lay claim on me. Through Your empowering grace, I faithfully promise that I will serve You as my Lord for the rest of my life.

If you just prayed this prayer of salvation, you are born again! You are a brand-new creation in Christ! Would you please let us know of your decision by going to **renner.org/salvation**? We would love to connect with you and pray for you as you begin your new life in Christ.

Scriptures for further study: John 3:16; John 14:6; Acts 4:12; Ephesians 1:7; Hebrews 10:19,20; 1 Peter 1:18,19; Romans 10:9,10; Colossians 1:13; 2 Corinthians 5:17; Romans 6:4; 1 Peter 1:3

Notes

Notes

_____

_____

_____

_____

_____

_____

_____

_____

_____

_____

_____

_____

_____

_____

_____

_____

_____

_____

_____

_____

_____

_____

_____

_____

_____

_____

_____

CLAIM YOUR FREE RESOURCE!

As a way of introducing you further to the teaching ministry of Rick Renner, we would like to send you FREE of charge his teaching, "How To Receive a Miraculous Touch From God" on CD or as an MP3 download.

In His earthly ministry, Jesus commonly healed *all* who were sick of *all* their diseases. In this profound message, learn about the manifold dimensions of Christ's wisdom, goodness, power, and love toward all humanity who came to Him in faith with their needs.

☑ **YES, I want to receive Rick Renner's monthly teaching letter!**

Simply scan the QR code to claim this resource or go to: **renner.org/claim-your-free-offer**

Connect

WITH US!